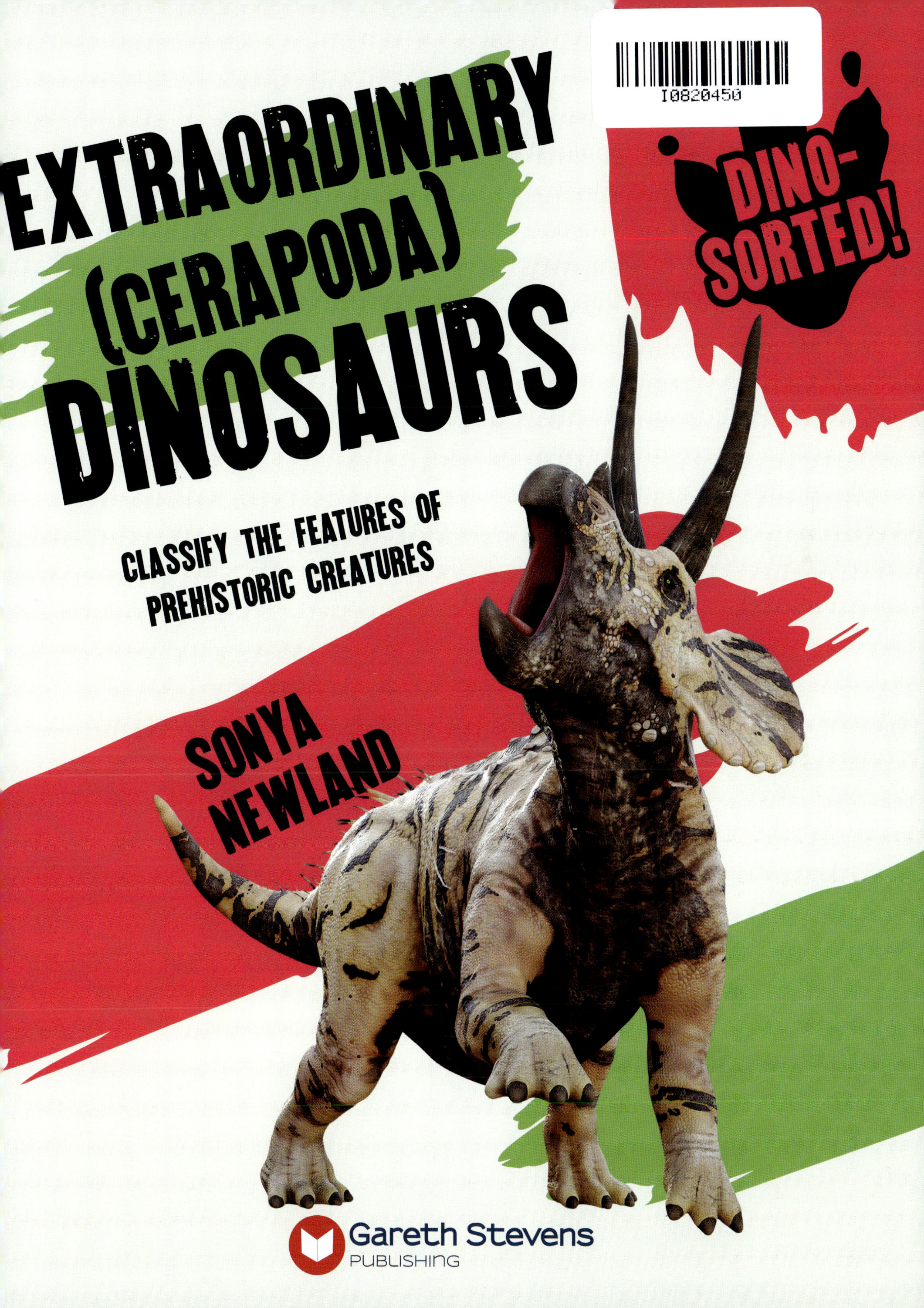

I0820450
EXTRAORDINARY
(CERAPODA)
DINOSAURS
DINO-
SORTED!
CLASSIFY THE FEATURES OF
PREHISTORIC CREATURES
SONYA
NEWLAND
Gareth Stevens
PUBLISHING

Please visit our website, www.garethstevens.com. For a free color catalog of all our high-quality books, call toll free 1-800-542-2595 or fax 1-877-542-2596.

Cataloging-in-Publication Data
Names: Newland, Sonya.
Title: Extraordinary dinosaurs / Sonya Newland.
Description: Buffalo, NY : Gareth Stevens Publishing, 2026. | Series: Dino-sorted! | Includes glossary and index.
Identifiers: ISBN 9781482473575 (pbk.) | ISBN 9781482473582 (library bound) | ISBN 9781482473599 (ebook)
Subjects: LCSH: Ornithischia--Juvenile literature. | Ornithischia--Classification--Juvenile literature. | Ceratopsidae--Juvenile literature.
Classification: LCC QE862.O65 N483 2026 | DDC 567.914--dc23

Published in 2026 by
Gareth Stevens Publishing
2544 Clinton St.
Buffalo, NY 14224

First published in Great Britain in 2021 by
The Watts Publishing Group

Credits
Editor: Sonya Newland
Designer: Dan Prescott, Couper Street Type Co.

The publisher would like to thank the following for permission to reproduce their pictures:

Alamy: Stocktrek Images, Inc. 6, 19b, 30, Alberto Paredes 11t, Friedrich Saurer 27t; Getty Images: Peter Bull 15b; Shutterstock: Herschel Hoffmeyer cover, 8–9, 19t, 28–29, Warpaint 4, 5l, 12–13, 15t, 16–17, 24–25, 26, Catmando 5r, 10, 11b, Denis Simonov 5b, YuRi Photolife 7, 22, Elenarts 9, 13, Michael Rosskothen 14, Daniel Eskridge 17b, 20–21, 25, Philippe Clement 17t, Ralf Juergen Kraft 18, AKKHARAT JARUSILAWONG 21, David Herraez Calzada 23t, Jean-Michel Girard 23b, Matis75 27b.

All design elements from Shutterstock.

Printed in the United States of America

CPSIA compliance information: Batch #CSGS26: For further information contact Gareth Stevens at 1-800-542-2595.

PRONUNCIATION GUIDE

Albertaceratops (al-berta-SERRA-tops)

Camptosaurus (KAMP-toe-SORE-us)

Centrosaurus (sen-troh-SORE-us)

Chasmosaurus (KAZ-mo-sore-us)

Dracorex (DRAY-koh-reks)

Edmontosaurus (ed-MON-toe-sore-rus)

Heterodontosaurus (HET-er-oh-DONT-oh-sore-us)

Hypsilophodon (hip-sih-LOH-foh-don)

Iguanodon (ig-WAH-no-don)

Lambeosaurus (lam-BEE-oh-SORE-us)

Leptoceratops (lep-toe-KER-ah-tops)

Lesothosaurus (le-SO-toe-SORE-us)

Micropachycephalosaurus (mike-row-pak-i-KEF-al-oh-SORE-us)

Ouranosaurus (oo-RAH-noh-SORE-us)

Pachycephalosaurus (pak-i-KEF-al-oh-SORE-us)

Pachyrhinosaurus (pack-ee-RINE-oh-SORE-us)

Parasaurolophus (pa-ra-sore-ROL-of-us)

Psittacosaurus (SIT-ak-oh-SORE-us)

Saurolophus (SORE-oh-LOAF-us)

Shantungosaurus (shan-TUN-go-sore-us)

Stegoceras (ste-GO-ser-as)

Tianyulong (te-AN-yoo-long)

Torosaurus (tor-oh-SORE-us)

Triceratops (tri-SERRA-tops)

CONTENTS

MEET THE

DINOSAURS ARE DIVIDED INTO CATEGORIES THAT SHARE CERTAIN FEATURES. THE CERAPODA BELONG TO A CATEGORY CALLED ORNITHISCHIA, OR "BIRD-HIPPED" DINOSAURS. THE CERAPODA THEMSELVES ARE SPLIT INTO TWO MAIN GROUPS—THE ORNITHOPODA AND THE MARGINOCEPHALIA.

Camptosaurus

Ornithopods ("bird-feet") were common from the Late Triassic Period. They were one of the most successful and long-lasting groups of dinosaurs. Within this group were several smaller families of dinosaurs, including heterodontosaurids, hypsilophodontids, iguanodontids and hadrosaurids. Ornithopods usually walked on two legs, but some may have moved on all fours when grazing.

The Marginocephalia ("fringed heads") emerged in the Jurassic Period and became more common throughout the Cretaceous Period. The two main groups were Pachycephalosauria, characterized by their thick skulls, and Ceratopsia, which had horns.

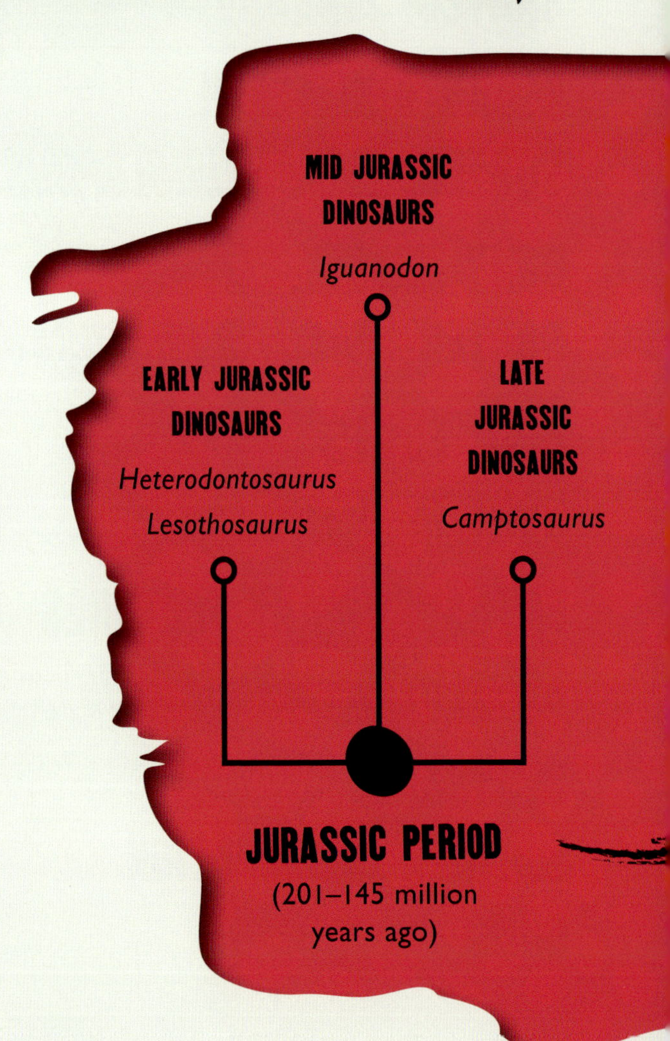

CERAPODA

Psittacosaurus

Centrosaurus

The Cerapoda were wiped out 66 million years ago in a mass extinction event that destroyed three-quarters of all life on Earth. Scientists believe that a huge asteroid crashed into Earth in the area that is now Mexico. The asteroid impact filled the air with deadly gas and dust for many years. This changed the climate so dramatically that few living things could survive.

EARLY CRETACEOUS DINOSAURS

Hypsilophodon
Ouranosaurus
Psittacosaurus

LATE CRETACEOUS DINOSAURS

Centrosaurus
Lambeosaurus
Parasaurolophus
Shantungosaurus
Torosaurus
Triceratops

CRETACEOUS PERIOD
(145–66 million years ago)

LITTLE AND LARGE

THE ORNITHOPODS OF THE EARLY JURASSIC PERIOD WERE QUITE SMALL ANIMALS. OVER TIME, SOME GROUPS EVOLVED TO BECOME MUCH LARGER. BUT THROUGHOUT ALL THEIR TIME ON EARTH, THE CERAPODA CAME IN MANY DIFFERENT SIZES.

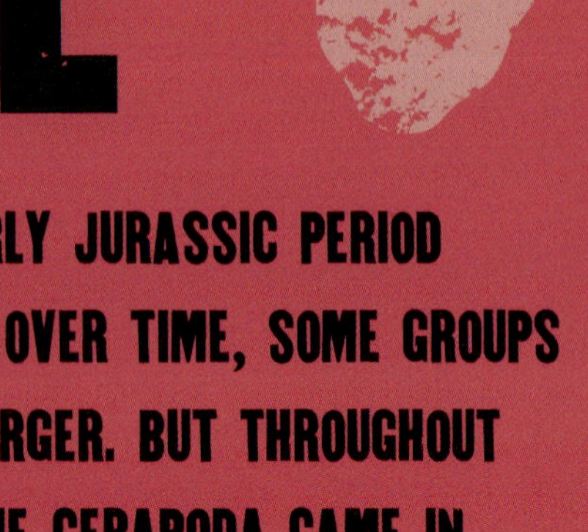

◀ Although only about 5.7 feet (1.75 m) long, *Heterodontosaurus* was one of the largest of the heterodontosaurids.

Some of the earliest heterodontosaurids, like the *Tianyulong*, were only about 2.5 feet (75 cm) from beak to tail tip! Hypsilophodontids were bigger, reaching up to 10 feet (3 m). The iguanodotids grew up to 30 feet (9 m). The hadrosaurids of the Late Cretaceous Period were the largest of all. Some grew to 50 feet (15 m)!

The early Ornithopods were small and light, which meant they could move quickly. They were bipeds–able to run on two legs. As they grew bigger, later species walked on four legs.

The Marginocephalia may have evolved from the Ornithopods. They generally had bigger, more barrel-like bodies than their early relatives. However, they still came in a wide range of sizes, from the 3.3 feet (1-m) *Micropachycephalosaurus* to species of Ceratopsia that could be more than 30 feet (9 m) long.

Members of the ceratopsid group ranged from 3.3 feet (1 m) to more than 30 feet (9 m) long. *Pachyrhinosaurus* could be 26 feet (8 m).

It's hard to say exactly how big or small different Cerapoda were. For some species, only a few bones have been found, so paleontologists have to estimate the sizes. Fossils may show us bigger or smaller species.

SORTED:

SHANTUNGOSAURUS

QUICK FACTS

PERIOD:
Late Cretaceous

LIVED IN:
China

HEIGHT:
50 feet (15 m)

WEIGHT:
3,500 pounds
(16,000 kg)

***SHANTUNGOSAURUS* LIVED IN WHAT IS NOW CHINA IN THE LATE CRETACEOUS PERIOD. SEVERAL MASSIVE DINOSAURS LIVED IN ASIA AT THIS TIME, BUT *SHANTUNGOSAURUS* WAS A MATCH FOR THEM ALL!**

BIG HEAD

Shantungosaurs had a long head. The largest skull found measures 5.3 feet (1.63 m)! At the end of its skull, *Shantungosaurus* had a bony beak. In its long jaws were 1,500 tiny, sharp teeth, which it used for slicing and chewing plant matter.

HUGE HADROSAUR

The hadrosaurids were the largest type of Cerapoda, but *Shantungosaurus* was the biggest of them all. Although paleontologists have not found a full skeleton, they have worked out its size from its leg bones. One thigh bone measured 5.6 feet (1.7 m)–as big as a bicycle!

TAIL

Shantungosaurus had a thick, powerful tail, which was carried stiffly above the ground. The heavy tail probably helped to balance the dinosaur as it walked.

GETTING AROUND

Like most of the bigger Ornithopods, *Shantungosaurus* walked on four legs almost all the time. However, despite being big and heavy, it may also have been able to lift up its front legs and run on its back ones.

DINOMIGHTY!

Shantungosaurus may have been the biggest dinosaur ever to have existed outside the group of giant sauropods.

SPECIALIZED LEGS AND FEET

THE CERAPODA WERE A MIXED GROUP. SOME WERE BIPEDS, WALKING ON TWO LEGS. OTHERS WERE QUADRUPEDS, MOVING ON ALL FOURS. THE LEGS AND FEET OF EACH SPECIES WERE ADAPTED TO THEIR SIZE, WEIGHT, AND ENVIRONMENT.

The small, light heterodontosaurids and hypsilophodontids walked upright on two legs. Their short arms had five-fingered hands that may have been used for digging up plant roots. They had long back legs. Some early Ornithopods had four toes, but most later species only had three.

◀ *Hypsilophodon* was small and light. It used its strong back legs to run at up to 25 miles (40 km) per hour.

Most baby hadrosaurids walked on two legs, but the large adults probably moved more easily on four. They had wide, short toes and fleshy pads on their feet, similar to the gigantic sauropods.

Evidence suggests that early iguanodontids moved on both two legs and four. They had unusual feet, with close, hoof-like second, third and fourth toes. Some experts think that these toes may have been fused together with skin.

Footprints, such as these three-toed Ornithopod tracks, can tell us a lot about this group of dinosaurs. For example, the distance between the footprints can suggest the size and speed of the dinosaur.

Like the early Ornithopods, the medium-sized Pachycephalosauria, such as *Stegoceras*, had wide hips, long back legs, and short front limbs.

One difference between the groups of Marginocephalia dinosaurs was in the way they walked. The Pachycephalosauria were bipeds. They had strong back legs and smaller front ones, which were more like arms. Early Ceratopsia had a similar body shape, but later species, such as *Triceratops*, were quadrupeds, with four thick, strong legs.

SORTED:

IGUANODON

IGUANODON WAS THE BIGGEST TYPE OF IGUANODONTID. IT WAS TWICE AS LONG AS THE LARGEST REPTILE ALIVE TODAY, THE SALTWATER CROCODILE!

QUICK FACTS

PERIOD:
Early Cretaceous

LIVED IN:
Europe, North Africa, North America

LENGTH:
33 feet (10 m)

WEIGHT:
8,800 pounds (4,000 kg)

DINOMIGHTY!

Iguanodon was only the second dinosaur ever to be discovered, in around 1820. When experts first examined the teeth, they thought they must be from a rhinoceros or a fish!

SLOW AND FAST

Like most other iguanodontids, *Iguanodon* could move on either two legs or four. It probably spent most of its time grazing on four legs, slicing leaves from trees and plants with its beak. Up on its hind legs, it could move at around 12 miles (20 km) per hour.

UNUSUAL HANDS

The bones in *Iguanodon*'s wrists were fused together. It had five fingers on each hand. The three middle fingers were close together, forming blunt claws, like a hoof. The outer finger was separate from the others and stuck out sideways.

USEFUL DIGITS

This outer finger was prehensile. That means it could be moved in a way that allowed it to wrap around things. This probably helped *Iguanodon* grab and hold plants. *Iguanodon*'s inner finger had a cone-shaped thumb spike, which may have been used as a weapon.

BEAKS AND TEETH

MOST CERAPODA HAD A TOOTHLESS, BONY BEAK AT THE FRONT OF THEIR SKULL. SOME HAD SHARP, NARROW BEAKS THAT WERE GOOD FOR BITING TOUGH PLANTS. OTHERS HAD WIDE, FLAT BILLS LIKE MODERN DUCKS. THE CERAPODA ALSO HAD MANY DIFFERENT SIZES AND SHAPES OF TEETH.

The Ornithopods grazed on plants that grew close to the ground. The beaks that first developed in the heterodontosaurids helped them dig up roots and other vegetation.

Ceratopsids like *Albertaceratops* developed with a hooked beak and rows of teeth at the back of the mouth for shearing plants.

▼ *Edmontosaurus* was one of the biggest duck-billed dinosaurs.

The hadrosaurids are also known as "duck-bills." They had long, wide, flat snouts that ended with a broad beak. The beak was made of keratin, which is the same material that hair and nails are made from.

Most Cerapoda were herbivores, feeding on different types of plants, fruit, and seeds. Some were omnivores, eating both plants and insects.

"Dont" means "teeth." Some Cerapoda groups were named after this feature! Heterodontosaurid means "different teeth." The group had tusk-like teeth and cheek teeth. Hypsilophodontid means "high ridge teeth." Iguanodontid means "iguana teeth."

◀ *Heterodontosaurus* had three different types of teeth. The small, sharp front teeth were used for biting. Two sets of tusk-like teeth were used for stabbing at leaves. The wider teeth at the back of the mouth were for chewing.

SORTED:

PARASAUROLOPHUS

THE LARGE HERBIVOROUS HADROSAURID *PARASAUROPHOLUS* LIVED IN WHAT IS NOW THE UNITED STATES AND CANADA. IT SPENT ITS LIFE GRAZING ON LEAVES, TWIGS, AND PINE NEEDLES.

QUICK FACTS

PERIOD:
Late Cretaceous

LIVED IN:
North America

LENGTH:
36 feet (11 m)

WEIGHT:
7,700 pounds (3,500 kg)

DINOMIGHTY!

Parasaurolophus's crest could probably emit very loud sounds over long distances, in the same way that whales and elephants communicate.

BROAD BEAK

Parasaurolophus's skull ended in a narrow, flat beak with a sharp edge. This was good for shearing off and gathering up mouthfuls of tough plant matter.

HEAD CREST

Parasaurolophus's most famous feature is its long, bony head crest. The crest extended from the top of the head and was as long as the skull itself. Some experts think it may have been used like an instrument to call out to other members of the herd. Others suggest it was a way of getting rid of body heat, similar to the way an elephant's ears carry heat away from its body.

TOUGH TEETH

Its jaws were packed with hundreds of small teeth, but only a few were used at a time. As *Parasaurolophus*'s front teeth wore away and fell out, the back teeth gradually shifted forward to take their place. The teeth were used to grind up plants in the mouth before swallowing.

BONY HEADS

PALEONTOLOGISTS HAVEN'T FOUND MANY PACHYCEPHALOSAURIA BONES, SO WE DON'T KNOW TOO MUCH ABOUT THEM WHEN COMPARED TO SOME OTHER DINOSAUR GROUPS. ONE THING WE DO KNOW, HOWEVER, IS THAT THE PACHYCEPHALOSAURS STOOD OUT FROM THE OTHER CERAPODA BECAUSE OF THEIR DISTINCTIVE THICK SKULLS.

In some species, the skull was shaped like a dome. But the skull could also be flat or wedge-shaped. In species such as *Stegoceras*, young dinosaurs had a thick, flat skull that got more domed as they became adults.

Dracorex (named after a character in the Harry Potter books) had a thick but flat skull. Some paleontologists think it may actually be a young *Pachycephalosaurus*.

The domes were often surrounded by bony lumps. In many dinosaurs, bumps and spikes appear in patterns, but in the Pachycephalosauria they seem to be randomly positioned on the head.

Some paleontologists now think that Pachycephalosauria fought by "flank-butting"–using their heads to hit each other on the side of the body.

Why did the Pachycephalosauria develop these thick skulls? Some think the dinosaurs head-butted each other in fights, so they evolved a thick dome to protect the brain. Or, the domes may have been a way for the Pachycephalosauria to recognize others of their own species.

The domes may also have been used for display. If this is the case, then they may have been brightly colored.

SORTED:

PACHYCEPHALOSAURUS

THE BIGGEST OF THE BONE-HEADED DINOSAURS, *PACHYCEPHALOSAURUS* IS FAMOUS FOR ITS HUGE DOMED SKULL. THIS FEATURE MIGHT HAVE PROTECTED THE DINOSAUR'S TINY BRAIN!

SKULL AND DOME

The dome that formed part of *Pachycephalosaurus*'s skull may not have been solid bone. Instead, it may have been softer inside, with holes in it like a sponge. This would have reduced the weight of the skull–but it would also have reduced its strength, making head-butting riskier.

BIG EYES

Fossil remains of *Pachycephalosaurus* show that this dinosaur had large eye sockets that faced forward in the skull. The size suggests that *Pachycephalosaurus* had big eyes and good eyesight compared to some dinosaurs. The fact that the eyes faced forward means that this dinosaur probably had binocular vision–that is, it could focus on an object with both eyes.

SPIKY SNOUT

All around the dome, *Pachycephalosaurus* had bony knobs and spikes. These extended right down the snout. Like other Cerapoda, *Pachycephalosaurus* had a pointed, horny beak at the end of its snout.

QUICK FACTS

PERIOD:
Late Cretaceous

LIVED IN:
North America

LENGTH:
26 feet (8 m)

WEIGHT:
6,600 pounds (3,000 kg)

DINOMIGHTY!

The dome of bone on *Pachycephalosaurus*'s head could be 10 inches (25 cm) thick. That's 20 times thicker than other dinosaur skulls!

NECK FRILLS

OF ALL THE TYPES OF CERAPODA, ONE GROUP HAD A PARTICULARLY DISTINCTIVE FEATURE. THE CERATOPSIA ARE FAMOUS FOR THEIR NECK FRILLS. THESE RANGED FROM VERY SMALL, BONY FRAMES IN EARLY DINOSAURS LIKE *LEPTOCERATOPS* TO THE GIGANTIC FRILLS ON *TOROSAURUS*.

Chasmosaurus was a medium-sized ceratopsid, but its neck frill was very long. It was broader at the ends than the front.

The frill was not a separate part of the skeleton. It was an extension of the bones in the neck. The frills came in all different shapes and sizes. Some had bony lumps or horns around the edge. The bone of the frill was covered in tough skin.

The covering of skin made the frills look solid. But, most frills had big holes in them, like windows in a frame. Bone is heavy. Having holes reduced the frill's weight.

Triceratops had an unusual neck frill, which was made of solid bone instead of having holes in the middle like the frills of most ceratopsids.

Paleontologists once thought neck frills were there to protect against predators. But neck frills were made of thin bone and had holes in them, so they would have broken under attack. Instead, the frill was probably used for display. The skin may have been brightly colored to help attract a mate.

As well as their frills, many ceratopsids had horns on their nose and above their eyes, like *Triceratops* (see page 27).

SORTED:

TOROSAURUS

***TOROSAURUS* WAS ONE OF THE BIGGEST CERATOPSIDS. ITS NAME MEANS "PERFORATED LIZARD." THINGS THAT ARE PERFORATED HAVE HOLES IN THEM, AND THIS DINOSAUR GOT ITS NAME BECAUSE OF THE HOLES IN ITS HUGE NECK FRILL.**

BIG FRILL

The huge fan-shaped neck frill stretched out from low on the back of *Torosaurus*'s skull. The frill was thinner than in some other species, such as *Triceratops*. This was probably to reduce the weight, as the frill was so large.

A GROWN-UP *TRICERATOPS*?

Some paleontologists think that *Torosaurus* may be the fully grown version of *Triceratops*. Others argue that they must be two different species, and use the neck frill as evidence. Even on the youngest *Torosauruses* discovered, the neck frill is bigger than *Triceratops*.

QUICK FACTS

PERIOD:
Late Cretaceous

LIVED IN:
North America

LENGTH:
25 feet (7.5 m)

WEIGHT:
8,800–13,200 pounds (4,000–6,000 kg)

HORNS

Behind the frill, *Torosaurus* had several pairs of small horns. It had two eye horns, like other ceratopsids, but its nose horn was shorter than in other dinosaurs.

DINOMIGHTY!

Torosaurus had one of the biggest skulls of any creature ever to have walked the Earth. With its huge frill, the skull was a massive 9 feet (2.8 m) long– that's about as long as you and a friend lying head to head!

BIG HEAD

Most ceratopsids had big heads– about one-fifth of their body size– but *Torosaurus*'s head was even bigger. The skull of this Cerapoda made up one-third of its body length!

EXTRAORDINARY FEATURES

WITH THEIR BEAKS, DOMED HEADS OR FRILLS, ALL THE SUB-GROUPS OF THE CERAPODA HAD THEIR OWN UNIQUE LOOK. BUT THESE WEREN'T THE ONLY EXTRAORDINARY FEATURES THIS CATEGORY OF DINOSAURS HAD.

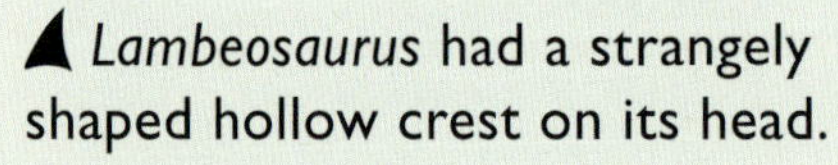

Lambeosaurus had a strangely shaped hollow crest on its head.

Some of the hadrosaurids had amazing head crests. These curved, bony tubes could sometimes be as long as the skull itself. The crest was covered in skin and there may also have been a web of skin between the crest and the neck.

A few Cerapoda, such as *Saurolophus*, had unusual spikes on their heads. This was especially strange in the hadrosaurid *Lambeosaurus*. This dinosaur had a spiky projection sticking out of its crest, giving the crest the shape of an axe!

Psittacosaurus was an early type of Ceratopsian. A fossil of this dinosaur was discovered that had an unusual tail feature–long bristles, or "filaments." No one knows the purpose of these long, tube-like structures, but some experts think they may have been used to attract a mate.

Psittacosaurus was covered in tiny scales.

The ceratopsids often had three horns–two above their eyes and one above the beak. They either had long eye horns and a short nose horn or vice versa. Males probably used them to fight predators and each other.

The horns on *Triceratops* could be 3.3 feet (1 m) long.

SORTED:

OURANOSAURUS

THIS EARLY CRETACEOUS DINOSAUR HAS PUZZLED SOME EXPERTS BECAUSE OF ITS UNUSUAL FEATURES. AT FIRST IT WAS CLASSIFIED AS AN IGUANADONTID, BUT NOW PALEONTOLOGISTS THINK IT MAY HAVE BEEN AN EARLY HADROSAURID.

QUICK FACTS

PERIOD:
Early Cretaceous

LIVED IN:
West Africa

LENGTH:
23 feet (7 m)

WEIGHT:
4,850–8,800 pounds (2,200–4,000 kg)

UNUSUAL HEAD

Ouranosaurus's head was bigger and its jaws longer than most iguanodontids. Along the top of its snout, above the eyes, were two wide bumps. These may have served the same purpose as the small horns on modern antelopes, which are used for display.

SAIL

Even more unusual is that *Ouranosaurus* has a "sail" on its back. This was a row of spines along the backbone, which were covered with skin. The sail may have been brightly colored to act as a warning to predators. *Ouranosaurus* is the only member of the Cerapoda to have this feature.

AN ORDINARY ORNITHOPOD?

In many ways *Ouranosaurus* was similar to others of its type. It was powerfully built, with long, strong back legs and smaller–but still strong–front legs. It had hoof-like hands and feet, and a thumb-spike like the iguanodontids.

DINOMIGHTY!

Ouranosaurus had unusually high nostrils. These may have come in handy when grazing in low, muddy areas, allowing it to crop the plants without getting mud up its nose!

GLOSSARY

ASTEROID – a large rock that forms in space and orbits the sun

BIPEDS – animals that walk on their two back legs

CARNIVORE – an animal that eats meat

CREST – a feature on the top of the head, made of bone, feathers, fur, or skin

EVOLVE – to change and develop gradually over time

FILAMENTS – very thin strands, like threads

FOSSIL – the shape of a plant or animal that has been preserved in rock for a very long time

FUSED – joined together

GRAZING – feeding slowly on low-lying vegetation

HERBIVORE – an animal that eats only plants and fruit

KERATIN – a fiber-like substance that hair, nails, claws, horns, etc. are made from

MASS EXTINCTION – the death of many living things

MATE – a reproductive partner

OMNIVORE – an animal that eats both plants and meat

ORNITHISCHIA – "bird-hipped" dinosaurs, one of the two main groups of dinosaurs

PALEONTOLOGIST – a scientist who studies dinosaurs and prehistoric life

PREDATOR – an animal that hunts and kills other animals for food

PREHENSILE – describing things that can move in a way that allows them to grasp objects

QUADRUPED – describing an animal that walks on four legs rather than two

SKULL – the bones that make up the head and face

SPECIES – a group of living things that are closely related and share similar features

SUB-GROUP – a group of animals within a larger category that have particular features in common

UNIQUE – not the same as anything else

FURTHER INFORMATION

BOOKS

Digging Up Dinosaur Fossils in North America
by Meg Greve (Little Mitchie, 2025)

Why? Dinosaurs
by Stephanie Warren Drimmer (National Geographic Kids, 2025.)

DRAW YOUR OWN

Use the information in this book to design a new Cerapoda. Remember to include the features of whatever sub-group you choose. Then give your dinosaur a name.

WEBSITES

www.amnh.org/exhibitions/dinosaurs-ancient-fossils/display-or-defense/my-what-a-big-skull-you-have
www.amnh.org/exhibitions/dinosaurs-ancient-fossils/display-or-defense/the-horned-dinosaurs
Get to know the Ceratopsians with these articles from the American Museum of Natural History.

www.nationalgeographic.com/animals/prehistoric/triceratops-horridus/
www.nationalgeographic.com/animals/prehistoric/pachycephalosaurus-wyomingensis/
Find out about *Triceratops* and *Pachycephalosaurus* in these fact files from National Geographic, and search for other Cerapoda.

INDEX